RELAXING MUSIC
FOR PIANO SOLO

ISBN 978-1-4803-9669-2

HAL•LEONARD®
CORPORATION
7777 W. BLUEMOUND RD. P.O. BOX 13819 MILWAUKEE, WI 53213

In Australia Contact:
Hal Leonard Australia Pty. Ltd.
4 Lentara Court
Cheltenham, Victoria, 3192 Australia
Email: ausadmin@halleonard.com.au

Visit Hal Leonard Online at
www.halleonard.com

AIR
from WATER MUSIC

By GEORGE FRIDERIC HANDEL
1685–1759

Slowly and stately

AIR ON THE G STRING
from ORCHESTRAL SUITE NO. 3

By JOHANN SEBASTIAN BACH
1685–1750

THE ASH GROVE

Old Welsh Air

Poco meno mosso

ARIA
from THE GOLDBERG VARIATIONS

By JOHANN SEBASTIAN BACH
1685–1750
BWV 899

Andante cantabile

AVE VERUM CORPUS

By WOLFGANG AMADEUS MOZART
1756–1791
K. 618

THE BAMBOO FLUTE

Chinese Folksong

BARCAROLLE
from THE TALES OF HOFFMANN

By JACQUES OFFENBACH
1819–1880

BEAUTIFUL DREAMER

By STEPHEN C. FOSTER

Slowly, like a lullaby

Poco meno mosso

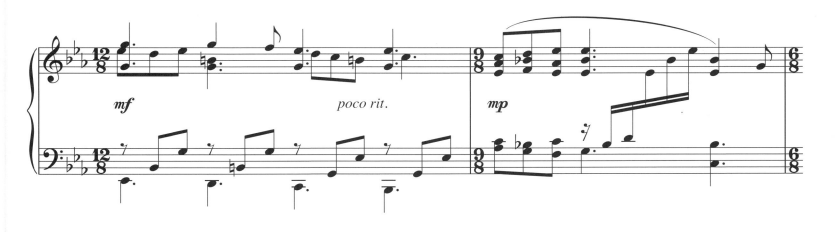

Tempo I

CANON IN D MAJOR

By JOHANN PACHELBEL
1653–1706

CLAIR DE LUNE
from SUITE BERGAMASQUE

By CLAUDE DEBUSSY
1862–1918

Andante très expressif

Tempo I

DANCE OF THE SPIRITS
from ORFEO ED EURIDICE

By CHRISTOPH WILLIBALD VON GLUCK
1714 –1787

EINE KLEINE NACHTMUSIK
(A Little Night Music)
Second Movement Excerpt, "Romance"

By WOLFGANG AMADEUS MOZART
1756–1791
K. 525

FLOW GENTLY, SWEET AFTON

Lyrics by ROBERT BURNS
Music by ALEXANDER HUME

GYMNOPÉDIE NO. 1

By ERIK SATIE
1866–1925

Lent et douloureux (slowly and mournfully)

With pedal

FÜR ELISE
(Bagatelle)

By LUDWIG VAN BEETHOVEN
1770–1827
WoO 59

HOW CAN I KEEP FROM SINGING

By REV. ROBERT LOWRY

JESU, JOY OF MAN'S DESIRING
from CANTATA NO. 147

By JOHANN SEBASTIAN BACH

Moderato

INTERMEZZO
from CAVALLERIA RUSTICANA

Py PIETRO MASCAGNI
1863–1945

Andante sostenuto

JUPITER
(Chorale Theme)
from THE PLANETS, Op. 32

By GUSTAV HOLST
1874–1934

Andante maestoso

LARGO
("Ombra mai fu")
from SERSE

By GEORGE FRIDERIC HANDEL
1685–1759

LONDONDERRY AIR

Traditional Irish

With motion, flowing

MAZURKA IN A MINOR
Op. 17, No. 4

By FRYDERYK CHOPIN
1810–1849

MEDITATION
from THAÏS

By JULES MASSENET
1842–1912

MINUET
from WATER MUSIC

By GEORGE FRIDERIC HANDEL
1685–1759

Tempo di Minuetto

MORNING
from PEER GYNT, Op. 46

By EDVARD GRIEG
1843–1907

PRELUDE IN C MAJOR
from THE WELL-TEMPERED CLAVIER, BOOK 1

By JOHANN SEBASTIAN BACH
1685–1750
BWV 846

Gracefully (♩ = 72)

NIMROD
from ENIGMA VARIATIONS, Op. 36

By EDWARD ELGAR
1857–1934

PASTORALE
from CHRISTMAS CONCERTO, Op. 6, No. 8

By ARCANGELO CORELLI
1653–1713

PIE JESU
from REQUIEM, Op. 48

By GABRIEL FAURÉ
1845–1924

PRELUDE IN B MINOR
Op. 28, No. 6

By FRYDERYK CHOPIN
1810–1849

PRELUDE IN E MINOR
Op. 28, No. 4

By FRYDERYK CHOPIN
1810–1849

RÊVERIE

By CLAUDE DEBUSSY
1862–1918

SAKURA
(Cherry Blossoms)

Traditional Japanese Folksong

SOLVEJG'S SONG

from PEER GYNT

By EDVARD GRIEG
1843–1907

THE SWAN
(Le cygne)
from CARNIVAL OF THE ANIMALS

By CAMILLE SAINT-SAËNS
1835–1921

SYMPHONY NO. 5 IN C-SHARP MINOR
Fourth Movement Excerpt
("Adagietto")

By GUSTAV MAHLER
1860–1911

TO A WILD ROSE

from WOODLAND SKETCHES

By EDWARD MacDOWELL
1860–1908

With simple tenderness (♩ = 88)

TRÄUMEREI
(Reverie)
from SCENES FROM CHILDHOOD

By ROBERT SCHUMANN
1810–1856
Op. 15, No. 7

WALTZ IN A-FLAT MAJOR
Op. 39, No. 15

By JOHANNES BRAHMS
1833–1897

Moderate Waltz tempo

THE WATER IS WIDE

Traditional